Table of Contents

Introduction

To start off on the right foot (and paw!) with your pup, he'll need to know what you expect from him. This will make him feel secure in his ability to meet the goals laid out for him going forward. The foundation of training should be based on positive reinforcement. Positive reinforcement is the process of giving a dog (or person!) a reward to encourage the behavior you want, like getting a pay check for going to work. The idea is not to bribe the behavior but to train it using something your dog values. Avoid using punishment such as leash corrections or yelling. Punishment can cause a dog to become confused and unsure about what is being asked of him. It is important to remember that we can't expect dogs to know what they don't know – just like you wouldn't expect a 2-year-old child to know how to tie his shoes. Patience will go a long way in helping your new puppy learn how to behave. Reinforcement can be anything your dog likes. Most people use small pieces of a "high value" food for training treats — something special — such as dried liver or even just their kibble. Lavish praise or the chance to play with a favorite toy can also be used as a reward. Dogs must be taught to like praise. If you give the dog a treat while saying "Good dog!" in a happy voice, he will learn that praise is a good thing and can be a reward. Some dogs also enjoy petting. Food is often the most convenient way to reinforce behavior. Puppies can begin very simple training starting as soon as they come home, usually around 8 weeks old. Always keep training sessions brief — just 5 to 10 minutes —and always end on a positive note. If your puppy is having trouble learning a new behavior, end the session by reviewing something he already knows and give him plenty of praise and a big reward for his success. If your puppy gets bored or frustrated, it will ultimately be counterproductive to learning. Sometimes the biggest challenge in dog training can be preventing a well-meaning family member from sabotaging the process. In some respects, teaching people how to train their dog is the equivalent of asking them to be the student and the teacher at the same time. And because consistency is key with dog training, it gets even more complicated when there are several people in the household. That's why it's important to include the children (and your spouse, for that matter) in every step of the process and to make sure everyone is following the rules in regard to training. If you do not have time to do all of the training yourself, no problem, as your dog's coach I can also be your dog's homeschool teacher. Day training is great for teaching or strengthening specific behavior skills such as loose leash walking, crate training, sit/down/settle/stay and more. As part of the day training package, once a week, I will teach you how to maintain and even strengthen your pet's skills. My goal for in home dog and puppy training is to help you not only solve your current dog behavior problems, but to also help you prevent future problems with a commitment to using the most positive strategies possible. As a training coach, I see my role as a teacher whose job it is to strengthen and inspire my clients' knowledge, skills, and problem-solving abilities. That goes for both my human and non-human students!

How To Teach A Dog To Come

You'll want to begin training a recall (come when called) in a quiet area and indoors. Sit with your puppy and say his name or the word "come." Each time you say "come/name," give your puppy a treat. He doesn't have to do anything yet! Just repeat the word and give a treat. Easy! Next, drop a treat on the floor near you. As soon as your puppy finishes the treat on the ground, say his name again. When he looks up, give him another treat. Repeat this a couple of times until you can begin tossing the treat a little further away, and he can turn around to face you when you say his name. Avoid repeating your puppy's name; saying it too often when he doesn't respond makes it easier for him to ignore it. Instead, move closer to your puppy and go back to a step where he can be successful at responding to his name the first time. Once your puppy can turn around to face you, begin adding movement and making the game more fun! Toss a treat on the ground and take a few quick steps away while calling your puppy's name. They should run after you because chase is fun! When they catch you, give them a lot of praise, treats or play with a tug toy. Coming to you should be fun! Continue building on these games with longer distances and in other locations. When training outside (always in a safe, enclosed area), it may be helpful to keep your puppy on a long leash at first. When your puppy comes to you, don't reach out and grab him. This can be confusing or frightening for some dogs. If your puppy is timid, kneel and face them sideways and offer him treats as you reach for the collar. Never call your dog to punish! This will only teach him that you are unpredictable, and it is a good idea to avoid you. Always reward your dog heavily for responding to his or her name, even if they have been up to mischief!

How To Teach a Dog Loose Leash Walking

In competition obedience training, "heel" means the dog is walking on your left side with his head even with your knee while you hold the leash loosely. Puppy training can be a little more relaxed with the goal being that they walk politely on a loose leash without pulling. Some trainers prefer to say "let's go" or "forward" instead of "heel" when they train this easy way of walking together. Whatever cue you choose, be consistent and

always use the same word.
Whether your puppy walks on your
left side or your right side is
completely up to you. But be
consistent about where you want
them so they don't get confused
and learn to zig zag in front of you.
First, make sure your puppy is
comfortable wearing a leash. This
can feel strange at first, and some
puppies may bite the leash. Give
your puppy treats as you put the
leash on each time. Then, stand
next to your puppy with the leash
in a loose loop and give him
several treats in a row for standing

or sitting next to your leg. Take one step forward and encourage him to follow by giving another treat as he catches up. Continue giving treats to your puppy at the level of your knee or hip as you walk forward. When he runs in front of you, simply turn the opposite direction, call him to you, and reward him in place. Then continue. Gradually begin giving treats further apart (from every step to every other step, every third step, and so on). Eventually your dog will walk happily at your side whenever he's on his leash.

Allow your dog plenty of time to sniff and "smell the roses" on your walks. When they've had their sniffing time, give the cue "Let's Go!" in a happy voice and reward them for coming back into position and walking with you.

How To Teach a Dog To Sit

There are two different methods for showing your puppy what "sit" means. The first method is called capturing. Stand in front of your puppy holding some of his dog food or treats. Wait for him to sit – say "yes" and give him a treat. Then step backwards or sideways to encourage him to stand and wait for him to sit. Give another treat as soon as they sit. After a few repetitions, you can begin saying "sit" right as he begins to sit. The next option is called luring.

Get down in front of your puppy, holding a treat as a lure. Put the treat right in front of the pup's nose, then slowly lift the food above his head. He will probably sit as he lifts his head to nibble at the treat. Allow him to eat the treat when his bottom touches the ground. Repeat one or two times with the food lure, then remove the food and use just your empty hand, but continue to reward the puppy after he sits. Once he understands the hand signal to sit, you can begin saying "sit" right before you give the hand signal.

Never physically put your puppy
into the sitting position; this can be
confusing or upsetting to some
dogs.

How To Teach a Dog To Stay

A puppy who knows the "stay" cue will remain sitting until you ask him to get up by giving another cue, called the "release word." Staying in place is a duration behavior. The goal is to teach your dog to remain sitting until the release cue is given, then begin adding distance. First, teach the release word. Choose which word you will use, such as "OK" or "free." Stand with your puppy in a sit or a stand, toss a treat on the floor, and say your word as he steps forward to get

the treat. Repeat this a couple of
times until you can say the word
first and then toss the treat AFTER
he begins to move. This teaches
the dog that the release cue means
to move your feet. When your dog
knows the release cue and how to
sit on cue, put him in a sit, turn and
face him, and give him a treat.
Pause, and give him another treat
for staying in a sit, then release
him. Gradually increase the time
you wait between treats (it can
help to sing the ABC's in your head
and work your way up the
alphabet). If your dog gets up

before the release cue, that's ok! It just means he isn't ready to sit for that long so you can make it easier by going back to a shorter time. Once your dog can stay in a sit for several seconds, you can begin adding distance. Place him in a sit and say "stay," take one step back, then step back to the pup, give a treat, and your release word. Continue building in steps, keeping it easy enough that your dog can stay successful. Practice both facing him and walking away with your back turned (which is more realistic). Once your dog can stay, you can gradually increase the distance. This is also true for the "sit." The more solidly he learns it, the longer he can remain sitting. The key is to not expect too much, too soon. Training goals are achieved in increments, so you may need to slow down and focus on one thing at a time. To make sure the training "sticks," sessions should be short and successful.

How to Teach a Dog to Lay Down

"Down" can be taught very similarly to "sit." You can wait for your dog to lie down (beginning in a boring, small room such as a bathroom can help) and capture the behavior by reinforcing your dog with a treat when he lies down, giving him his release cue to stand back up (and encouragement with a lure if needed) and then waiting for him to lie down again. When he is quickly lying down after standing up, you can begin

saying "down" right before he does
so. You can also lure a down from
a sit or stand by holding a treat in
your hand to the dog's nose and
slowly bringing it to the floor. Give
the treat when the dog's elbows
touch the floor to start. After a few
practices, begin bringing your
empty hand to the floor and giving
the treat AFTER he lies down.
When he can reliably follow your
hand signal, begin saying "down"
as you move your hand. Keep
training sessions short and fun.
End each session on a positive
note. If you feel your dog is having

a difficult time learning or being "stubborn," evaluate the speed of your training and the value of your rewards. Do you need to slow down and make the steps easier, or does your dog need a bigger paycheck for a harder exercise?

Tips for Getting your Dog to Come to You – Every Time You Call!

"Come" is the most important word that you will teach your dog, and if it is trained using positive reinforcement and play, you are more likely to have a successful, reliable recall. Maintaining a solid recall is a lifelong training effort that includes enthusiasm, consistency, and most importantly, rewards – lots and lots of rewards!

Before You Begin:

Never use your recall cue to call your dog to you for something negative, such as a reprimand, isolation, to get their nails clipped, or anything else your dog finds to be negative. Always make sure it is fun and positive every time they run to you. If you have inadvertently already been calling your dog for things that he or she considers unpleasant, then just change your command and start training all over so your dog learns that coming to you is the best thing in the world! So, if you need to get your dog for something he considers unpleasant (such as a bath or nail trim), do not use your "come" command – just go get the puppy without associating a word with it.

Teaching the Recall:

Start slowly by practicing at home with minimal distractions and plenty of fun or yummy rewards, like toys and treats. First, show your dog a high-value treat as you move backwards and say the dog's name in a bright, happy tone. If the puppy runs straight to you, reward with several small treats. Be very exciting and make the puppy understand what great fun it is to run to you. As he comes to you, give him several treats AND praise AND petting AND play. Once your dog is running consistently straight to you, you can name the behavior (come, here, etc.). When going outside to practice, there will be more distractions, so always keep your dog on a leash or safety long line until he has been trained more thoroughly, and don't forget to use high value treats!

Collar Grabs:

Practice grabbing your dog's collar when he comes to you, just before you give him the treat. This will avoid your dog taking the treat and run away to play the game again. It will also make your dog associate a "collar grab" with a good thing and not something to run away from and avoid.

Reinforcing the Recall:

The key to success is building a great relationship with your dog. You must try to be "Be the Very Best, Most Interesting Human Ever in the History of the Entire World" each and every time you call your dog to come. Also remember to never, ever reprimand your dog after you ask them to come to you! This rule applies to every recall and means that no matter how many times you call or how long it takes for your dog to get to you, he gets huge rewards once he gets to you. Have your dog randomly check in with you many times while at play, especially with other dogs. Just call them to you, give them a treat and then release them back to play. That way, "come!" is not associated with leaving or being leashed.

A New Way of Teaching Sit – From The Down

When people start training their dogs, "sit" is usually where they start. It's an easy basic. I've taught lots of dogs to sit! Then I got a retired racing greyhound.None of the usual methods worked; his back legs were pillars of unbending granite. No amount of luring or tricks would get him to fold those knees into a sit. He was, however, happy to do a down and learned that cue in minutes. Therefore, a solid "down" is the key to learning "sit" using this method. You are going to lure the dog up into a sit from a down.

Keep the sessions short and frequent. For this dog, sitting is awkward. Don't drill him; training should be fun! Have handy lots of your dog's favorite treats, cut into small, bite-size pieces. It should be something special that he really, really wants. Put him in the down position on a rug so he'll be comfortable and have traction. He won't be able to push up on a slick floor. Hold the treat above his nose to lure his head into looking up. Position it so that he doesn't move forward. If his back end comes up, quickly and calmly get him back down. Mark any upward movement of his front half with "Yes!" and reward. Don't say "sit" yet; just mark the desired behavior with an enthusiastic "Yes!" and give the treat. Release him after each partial sit, play with him a little, then reposition him in the down and try again. Soon he will be reaching, even getting his chest off the ground a little. Yes! Reward this! But no treat if the rear comes up. Any movement at all in the right direction should be lavishly rewarded. This is a good place to stop for a while. Remember, short, fun sessions. With the lure, encourage him to reach farther. With the front feet, he will start pushing himself up into a sit, little by little to reach the treat, because it's so delicious. Let him nibble the treat that is tightly gripped in your fist to guide him upward. Continue treating him and praising as long as he's moving up and keeping his rear on the ground. Reward lavishly every tiny bit he goes up, no matter how small. Two times is enough for each session, and scooting up even an inch is success. You might get lucky, but don't expect a full sit after the first lesson! Soon you should be luring him up to a pretty decent sit. Now you can start using the cue "Sit!" when he gets to the right position, praising and rewarding. Keep using the rug, even after your dog is pushing up right away. Practice the sit from a down, using the cue "sit," until he has it down solid. He should be pushing up to a sit right away for the treat and can connect the position to the word. When he scoots right into a sit on cue without being lured, it's time to try the sit from a stand. By this time he knows what the word means, and that he can indeed bend his knees, so let him know you have a treat and ask for the sit. Reward and let him know he's the best dog in the world. Once your dog gets the hang of it, move to different surfaces, such as grass, the sidewalk, the kitchen floor. Obviously there won't always be a nice rug available. Be prepared with treats each time you try a new surface until he's comfortable with it. If it seems that this requires an awful lot of treats, just remember that sitting can be difficult for Greyhounds, other sight hounds with similar builds, and some adult dogs that have never learned to sit. It isn't painful; it's just something that they haven't been taught. You can use intermittent rewards and praise once your dog knows what to do. Congratulations! You've taught your dog to sit!

How to Teach Your Kids to Train the Dog

Sometimes the biggest challenge in dog training can be preventing a well-meaning family member from sabotaging the process. In some respects, teaching people how to train their dog is the equivalent of asking them to be the student and the teacher at the same time. And because consistency is key with dog training, it gets even more complicated when there are several people in the household. That's why it's important to include the children (and your spouse, for that matter) in every step of the process and to make sure everyone is following the rules in regard to training.

- Let them be involved. I once had a student who wouldn't let her kids near her puppy that would be competing in obedience. The children weren't even allowed to talk to the dog because she didn't want them to "mess up the training." Personally, I found that including my kids in the training process brought us closer together as a family. A child as young as 5 years old could understand how to ask a dog to sit before giving him a treat. And since you're never leaving your young kids and dogs alone together without parental supervision, you'll be able to help him follow through on training properly.

- Turn your back on jumping. Teach everyone in the house and regular visitors that when they approach your dog while he's in a pen or behind a gate and he jumps up, they are to turn their backs to him. After the dog has settled down, they can turn around and see what his choice is. If he sits, they can give him a treat. If not, repeat the process. Also, by having your kids teach this technique to guests, they will see how challenging it is to convince other people to follow directions.

Give kids their own commands. Kids can be unpredictable and inconsistent, and it's difficult to retrain a word after a dog has confused its meaning. That's why I give my kids different words to train the dog. My dogs learn to come to me on the word "here," and they learn to stay on the word "wait." But I told my kids that they were going to train the words "come" and "stay." That way, they wouldn't use my words and would focus on theirs.

- Teach children how to use treats and praise. It's important that kids learn how to teach their dog that they are just as exciting as a treat. I remember having this conversation with my son when he was little. He said that the puppy only wanted to be around him when he was holding dog treats. I told him that I was going to let him in on a really important dog-training secret: In order to make this puppy want him as much as the cookie, he had to teach him to do something in order to get the cookie. So waiting for him to sit and then giving him a cookie (or opening a door or throwing a ball) made him just as valuable

to the puppy, because
suddenly he was the
gatekeeper of everything the
puppy wants.

Why Do Dogs Kick After They Poop?

Dogs have several behaviors that would seem odd if a human were to do them but are completely normal in the canine world. Kicking the hind legs after pooping is one of these behaviors that may appear to have no purpose, but, in reality, there are reasons why your dog may be doing it.

Marking Territory

Dogs have scent glands in the bottom of their feet that they use to mark their territory. Domesticated dogs don't necessarily need these glands, but their ancestors used them to claim their domain. The scent glands contain invisible scent-marking chemicals called pheromones and these chemicals are a dog's calling card or identifier. Urine and anal gland secretions also contain pheromones and may be used to mark territory. Other dogs will

smell the pheromones after a dog
kicks, even though humans cannot,
and will be able to tell that the
poop belongs to someone else. It
could be used as a warning signal
for territorial dogs or as a sign that
a dog is ready to mate. You may
even notice your dog kicking like
this after sniffing another dog's
poop or urine. This may be in an
effort to cover the other dog's
scents with their own pheromones.
This kicking behavior is a natural
form of communication for dogs,
even if there is no longer a need
for it as a domesticated canine,

and it isn't something to be concerned about. Dogs that tend to be more dominant, however, are often the ones that do the most aggressive kicking after pooping. If you live in a multi-dog household, you may notice that some of your dogs hardly kick while others put on quite a display.

Burying or Spreading Waste

Another reason why your dog may be kicking its feet after pooping is because it could be trying to bury its waste. This behavior is more commonly associated with cats, but dogs may try and bury their waste too. The act of burying waste isn't done because a dog is trying to hide something, though, but rather to spread the scent of their poop further. Kicking up dirt and covering it brings more attention to the feces so it is another way a dog marks its territory after pooping. On a rare occasion, a dog may actually try to bury its feces if it feels threatened and is trying to hide its presence, but this is more common in wild canines.

Wiping Paws

Some dogs do not enjoy having dirty paws, so if they get something on them after pooping they may be kicking in an attempt to wipe their paws off. They don't like the feeling of the dirt or debris on their paws and are simply trying to flick it off, much like they would rub their face on the ground if they feel as though something is on it. Although kicking can be a sign of discomfort or an attempt to get something off paws, when this is done only after the act of pooping,

it is more likely to be associated
with one of the other two reasons
above.

Can You Stop Your Dog From Kicking After They Poop?

While your dog may mean well
when it kicks after pooping, many
dog owners don't enjoy the
damage it causes to their
landscaping. However, where
possible, the kicking behavior your
dog exhibits should not be
discouraged since it is natural and

instinctive. There are some management techniques you can apply, however, to limit the damage it may be causing to your grass. Walking your dog on a leash off of your property is the best way to protect your landscaping. This avoidance method will still allow your dog to kick after pooping, but since it will be down the street or in a public dog walking area, you won't be upset if the grass gets ruined. Another option is to train them or limit them to pooping in a specific area like a dog run. Designate an area for your dog to go potty and instead of using nice grass, put down river rocks, pebbles, or mulch so your dog won't do any damage. This way your dog can do what it does best and you don't need to worry about it. Attempting to stop this behavior by yelling at your dog after pooping could result in your dog becoming fearful of pooping around you and it can damage the bond of trust between you. It may start pooping in the house in an attempt to do it in secret or develop diarrhea due to the stress of being yelled at.

Why Dogs Roll In Poop and Other Stinky Things

It never fails: after giving your puppy a bath so he looks and smells lovely, he runs outside and rolls in poop. Dogs and puppies live through their noses, and as many dog owners can tell you, pungent scents prompt rolling behavior. Think of it as a scent ecstasy, similar to what cats experience when exposed to catnip. When a dog finds what he considers an attractive odor, he rolls to rub his shoulders, back and neck into the offering. We don't know for sure why dogs are drawn to roll around in things that smell repugnant to humans. But there are a few possible explanations.

Dogs Have a Nuanced Sense of Smell

It's no secret that dogs' noses are much more sensitive than humans' But it's not just that dogs' sense of smell is acuter than ours, dogs actually can detect more layers of scent. For instance, when a skunk sprays a rose bush, a human only smells the skunk's aftermath since it's a more recent and stronger odor than the rose bush's own scent. But if a dog sniffed the same rose bush, it would be able to smell both the skunk and the roses and probably myriad other odors as well. This is likely an evolutionary trait that helped dogs communicate with their packs when wild canines roamed the earth. "Perfuming" himself with such scents may allow the dog to carry the smelly message home, so other dogs in the pack can learn all about a potential food source. Since many species of wild dogs were scavengers, they'd be drawn to smells such as rotting carcasses (which, not to be too graphic, smell not unlike feces).

Dogs May be Trying to Mark Their Territory

It's well known that pack and territorial animals will mark their territory by urinating on it. This scent lets other rival packs know to avoid a given area unless they want to fight for it. A wild dog or wolf rolling in poop (or other animal matter) may be trying to override another animal's scent, or intentionally leaving its own scent as a warning. Again, not the clearest explanation for why pet dogs engage in this behavior, but it at least provides some evolutionary clues.

Dogs Rolling in Poop May be Using Camouflage

Like their predecessors, pet dogs may roll in poop and other unpleasant-smelling material in order to mask their own scent. Wolves, especially, would not want a potential prey animal such as a deer to be able to smell them coming. If its own smell was camouflaged with the smell of poop, the predator would have an easier time hunting its prey.

Sometimes, Dogs Just Get Bored

It's also well-established that a bored or understimulated puppy will engage in destructive behaviors like chewing and digging. So it's not too much of a stretch to think that rolling in poop may be a sign you need to pay more attention to your dog and keep him occupied with other, less smelly hobbies.

Why Is My Dog Licking His Paws?

You have probably noticed your dog licking his paws from time to time. It's normal for dogs to lick their paws occasionally, but excessive paw-licking may be a sign of a problem. If you see your dog frequently licking his paws, it's time to take some action.

Why Dogs Lick Their Paws

Dogs typically lick their paws as a part of self-grooming. If your dog is a fastidious groomer, you may notice him licking his paws after meals, while settling down for a nap, or after coming in from outdoors, after meals. Even dogs that don't do a lot of self-grooming will occasionally clean their paws. If you notice your dog licking his paws every once in a while, then there's probably nothing to worry about. It is not normal if your dog seems to be licking his paws frequently or aggressively. This is usually a sign of a health problem or a behavior issue.

Health Problems and Paw-Licking

If you think your dog's paw-licking is abnormal, the first step is to determine if there is a health problem with the paws. Dogs often lick their paws excessively if they are itchy, irritated, or painful. A paw injury or foreign object may explain a sudden onset of paw-licking. The dog may have stepped on something that causes discomfort, like a sharp object or hot pavement. Or, he could have been stung or bitten by an insect or another animal. There may even be an object or substance stuck to his paws and he needs help removing it. Foreign objects like splinters or grass awns can get embedded in the paws and cause irritation. Another possibility is that your dog has an abnormal growth on one of his paws, such as a cyst or a tumor. Or, your dog may have arthritis or an injury to the soft tissue or bones of the paw. The latter may not be something you can see with the naked eye. if your dog is focusing on one paw more than the others, then it's more likely a paw injury, foreign object, or growth. However, these problems can easily affect more than one paw at a time. Allergies often cause itching or irritation of the paw pads, causing a dog to lick their paws for relief. Many dogs have allergies that make the paws itch. Food allergies are especially known to cause paw itching. It's not uncommon for dogs to develop bacterial or fungal infections of the paws. These infections may occur for unknown reasons. However, sometimes they are secondary to allergies. When a dog frequently licks his paws, they stay damp and are more susceptible to bacteria and fungi. External parasitic infections like fleas or mange or hookworms also tend to make the paws very itchy, leading to excessive licking.

What to Do If Your Dog Is Licking Their Paws Too Much

If it feels like your dog is constantly licking their paws, begin by taking a close look at the paws. Inspect the tops and bottoms of the feet, the toenails and nail beds, and the spaces in between the digits. Look for foreign objects, cuts, bruises, bleeding, swelling, redness, crusting, scabs, discharge, broken nails, and anything else that looks abnormal. Administer first aid if necessary. Note that excessive licking often causes saliva stains on the hair around the paws. This rust-colored staining is easiest to see where the hair is a light color. It's important to contact your veterinarian whether or not the paws look abnormal to you. Your vet needs to rule out health problems before you start trying to address a behavior issue. If your dog has a problem that may need advanced testing or treatment, your vet may refer you to a specialist, like a veterinary dermatologist or a veterinary surgeon. If there is no physical reason for your dog to lick their

paws excessively, then there's a
chance your dog has developed a
behavior issue.

Behavioral Problems and Paw-Licking

If all health concerns have been
ruled out, it is most likely that your
dog is licking their paws for
behavioral reasons. It may be as
simple as boredom. Or, it could be
a sign of stress, fear or anxiety. The
licking might have started due to
boredom, and then developed into

a habit that has become relaxing or satisfying for your dog. In severe cases, your dog may have obsessive-compulsive tendencies that lead them to obsessively lick their paws. A simple way to address behavioral paw-licking is to distract your dog. Take them for more walks, play with them more often, and offer them toys to hold their focus. Don't scold them for licking, but don't reward them with treats either. If the licking continues, consider behavior modification techniques to help your dog. Consult a dog trainer or behaviorist for help.

Tips

Behavioral modification to stop paw licking and chewing takes time, patience, and consistency. Consider a bitter-tasting topical product that is pet-safe to discourage licking. If this does not work, a physical restraint like an e-collar may be necessary. If additional behavior help is needed, consider working with a dog trainer, animal behaviorist, or a veterinary specialist in behavior

Help Your Dog Get Over Its Fearing Strangers

Some dogs suffer extreme fear of strangers. They cower, tremble, and try to hide from any new person they meet. While it's not unheard of for dogs to be afraid of strangers, the ideal reaction is one of open friendliness, not hiding or running away. If your dog is excessively fearful around

strangers, it's a good idea to
understand the reasons why so
you can help it get past its fear.

Reasons for Fear

There are several reasons why
your dog may be scared of people
it doesn't know. One possibility is
its genetics. A shy or timid dog is
more likely to produce skittish
offspring. A dog that has a general
fear of all strangers—rather than a
specific fear of men or children, for
example—may be genetically

predisposed to being fearful. A lack of proper socialization as a puppy is another reason some dogs fear strangers. Puppies that don't have a chance to meet a wide variety of people are more likely to develop a fear of people they don't know. Dogs with a history of abuse may also be afraid of strangers. If you're aware of a history of abuse, then you can better understand why your dog fears strangers.

Easing the Fear

A dog's fear of strangers should be managed very carefully. All dogs react differently when they're afraid. One dog may simply cower in a corner in the presence of a stranger. Another dog may react by growling or snapping. Teaching a dog not to be afraid usually takes lots of time and consistent training. You may expect your dog to react fearfully toward strangers. This can result in your tensing up or tightening your hold on its leash. Try to stay friendly, relaxed, and upbeat when you and your dog meet new people. Some dogs never learn to fully accept strangers, but you may be able to alleviate your dog's fear to some extent. Do not force your fearful dog to meet people or accept pets if it does not want them as this can sometimes lead to fear biting. Depending on your dog's reaction, working with a certified dog behaviorist to help identify cues and management strategies to practice is be very helpful. Every dog learns and adjusts at its own pace. This process can take weeks, months, or even longer.

Prepare New Visitors

Whenever anyone new comes to visit, have the person completely ignore the dog. The visitor should not attempt to pet or make eye contact with the dog. Have some treats on hand for your visitor to gently toss on the floor close to your dog during the visit. With consistent application, your fearful dog may slowly begin to associate strangers with rewards. Some dogs are more afraid of men than women. If you notice your dog tensing up, whining, or growling around strangers of a particular gender, you can prepare your guests accordingly. Allow your dog to approach a stranger on its terms. Depending on the severity of your dog's fear, it may quickly warm up to a stranger and allow petting and handling, or it may need several visits to warm up to a new person. Some dogs with very severe behavior may need to go to a comfortable place in the home away from visitors where they can rest and not be anxious when visitors come. If you have noticed growling or any form of aggression from your dog, it is very important to work with a certified dog behaviorist to help figure out triggers and if your pet can act safely with visitors. You never want to put visitors or your dog in a situation where someone may get bitten. Once your dog does approach, the person should continue to avoid eye contact and make slow, non-threatening movements. Never force your dog to accept handling by a stranger, especially a child. If a dog is pushed too far out of its comfort zone and not allowed to get away, it may resort to biting. Because dogs that are afraid of strangers may bite out of fear, it's your job to make sure that everyone stays safe around your dog. This may mean putting your dog in a different room when certain people visit.

Keep Things Stress-Free

Give your dog a space of its own. It helps if you have a spot, such as a quiet room, for the dog where it knows it will be left alone. A crate makes a perfect place for your dog to escape to when it gets too anxious. Applying a thunder shirt or spraying calming doggy pheromones in its safe spot may also be helpful. If your pet is in a safe spot, do not allow people to go in there and pull it out or even try to pet it as the dog must have an area where it can be left alone and unbothered. Removing your dog from potentially fearful situations is perfectly acceptable especially if it will help keep both visitors and your dog safe. Safe spots for dogs do not need to be a large space; a corner of a comfortable, quiet room where your dog can curl up with its favorite toy or blanket will serve just fine. Make sure no one goes in this area without checking first; the dog must feel like it won't be interrupted or surprised to feel safe.

Veterinary Care and Pharmaceuticals

Discussing your pet's fear with your veterinarian is important as he or she can help guide you on tactics you can use at home and discuss if medication may be warranted. Veterinarians may even recommend a consult with a boarded veterinarian behaviorist who specializes in dogs with behavioral problems such as fear. Or he or she may recommend at-home training with a certified dog trainer (CDPDT).

Obedience Training

Obedience training can be very helpful in managing fearful behavior and relieving some of your dog's stress. Because a severe fear of strangers can lead to aggressive behavior, including growling, snapping, and biting, it can be useful to work with a dog trainer or behaviorist to come up with a plan to deal with your dog's fear of strangers. Finding a certified dog trainer to work with you and your fearful pet is helpful at any stage. Typically the sooner a trainer is involved with a fearful pet, the better. CDPDT trainers can approach situations objectively and teach you how to help your fearful pet safely interact in the environment. For some pets, they may set up a specific desensitization and training plan. For others, they may determine that the best way to keep a pet and others safe is to remove them from potential fear-inducing situations. And yet for other situations, a trainer may recommend a modality such as a wire basket muzzle that can help

limit biting while still allowing a pet
to pant and drink water. Basket
muzzles (or any muzzle) are best
used as guided by a certified
trainer or veterinarian who can
assure they are only used for
limited periods, in appropriate
situations, and with a proper fit.
Muzzles are never to be used for
punishment and nylon or cloth
muzzles are not recommended
outside a veterinary office because
dogs can not pant well through
them, which can lead to emergent
situations. Fearful pets can provide
challenges for owners but

practicing patience, smart management of your pet and seeking help from trainers and veterinarians can be instrumental in helping fearful pets manage their fears.

How to Solve Your Dog's Fear of Children

Dogs and kids make a great combination under the right circumstances and often form lifelong bonds. When a dog is afraid of children, though, it's not always safe to bring them together. It's actually fairly common for dogs to be wary of kids (and vice versa), and if your dog is among them, there are ways you can address its fears to help prevent confrontations.

Why Do Dogs Fear Children?

There are two major reasons why dogs may develop a fear of children. A lack of early socialization:

Dogs who aren't exposed to children as puppies may become fearful when they meet them later in life. When they encounter children for the first time as adult dogs, they may be extremely frightened by the unfamiliar size, smells, noises, and movements of children.

The aftermath of a negative experience: Dogs may also develop a fear of children after a painful or unsettling interaction. Young children often have a tendency to pull tails, grab handfuls of fur, steal toys, and even poke eyes. Some dogs are tolerant of children's poking and prodding. Other dogs may develop a fear of children after only one bad experience.

Next Steps

Because it's unlikely that a dog will go through its entire life without ever meeting a child, it's important that you work on managing your dog's fear. This is not only for the sake of your dog; it is also important to prevent dog bites and other injuries to children.

Fortunately, there are a number of things you can do to minimize your dog's fear around children.

Socialize Early

If you have just brought home a puppy, start socializing it with children right away. Puppies got through a peak socialization period at around 8 to 12 weeks of age, during which time they should be exposed to as many different situations as possible. Keep in mind that all interactions should be supervised and kept as positive, upbeat, and calm as possible. Working on socialization now may save you lots of time, effort, and anguish later on. Many people have pets before they have children. Then they're surprised when their dogs growl or snap at the new infant or toddler. This can be a heartbreaking situation for the dog owner and the dog, but the key to preventing the problem is early and frequent socialization.

Take Precautions

Never leave your dog unsupervised with children. This should be the rule for all dogs but especially for a dog who's afraid of children or if it's not known whether the dog is afraid. Prematurely leaving them alone to play puts both the dog and the children in a bad position that can result in even greater fear in the dog or an injury to the children. When a fearful dog (or a new dog) is around children, don't take your eyes off them for a second and be ready to separate them at the first sign that the dog is becoming uncomfortable. Don't force your dog to make friends with a child. Making your dog stand still while a child approaches it or pets it is asking for trouble. If a fearful dog is pushed too far beyond its comfort zone, aggression can be the result, particularly if it is prevented from leaving the stressful situation. Don't put your dog in a position where it feels forced to defend itself.

Provide a Safe Space

All dogs need a quiet, safe space where they can be left alone. If your dog is afraid of children, make sure it has a safe, quiet spot it can get to when children are around but that the children cannot access. If your dog is crate trained, a crate makes a perfect hiding spot. Don't allow children anywhere near your dog's safe area.

Establish Rules

If you have children and a fearful dog living in the same household, it's important that your children have rules to follow. They should never be allowed to interact with the dog unsupervised, and they should know never to try to take the dog's toys or approach the dog while it's eating or sleeping. It's also important that you spend time teaching your children the right way to interact with dogs. This includes how to touch your dog with gentle petting rather than poking, prodding, and pulling.

Train Your Dog

Desensitization is the process of gradually increasing your dog's interactions with children to make it more comfortable with them. Because a fearful dog can become aggressive, it's important to handle desensitization carefully. For example, you can start by tossing your dog a few treats when it sees children from a distance and remains relaxed. Very slowly over the course of several days, weeks, or months (depending on the severity of the fear), you can decrease the distance between your dog and children as long as no signs of stress appear, all the while handing out treats and praise. Never punish a dog who is reacting out of fear as that only confirms to the dog that it had a good reason to be afraid. Find a veterinary behaviorist or reputable dog trainer with experience in dealing with fearful dogs who uses only positive reinforcement. Because dogs who are afraid of children run the risk of biting, it is often beneficial to call in a professional. A trainer or behaviorist can help you implement a desensitization program and get results more quickly and safely than you might otherwise.

Be Patient

These things can take a long time, and your dog may never fully accept children. However, with patience and perseverance you should be able to minimize its fear and prevent dog bites.

10 Best Medium-Sized Dogs for Kids

If you have kids in the family, you might wonder which dog breeds are best. Tiny dogs are generally not recommended for families with young children because they are too delicate, and very large breeds can unintentionally knock over your little ones. Enter the medium-sized dog. Not too big and not too small, medium dog breeds (in general, those weighing between 20 to 50 pounds) are a great choice for families with children of all ages. Even with breeds that are good with kids, most pet experts recommend waiting until your youngest child is five years old before welcoming a dog into the family. By that age, most children have a better handle on impulse control and are more capable of both understanding and following the rules for interacting with the dog. No matter what, an adult should always supervise all interactions between kids and dogs of any breed, just to be on the safe side. Your new dog will be part of your life for the next decade or longer, possibly until your kids are grown and out of the house. Take your time now to choose the best breed for your family, and teach your kids how to interact with dogs safely.

Here, we've rounded up 12 medium breeds that are known for living happily with kids.

Don't forget that although dogs of a certain breed are more likely to share similar traits, every dog is an individual. They all have their own unique characteristics and personalities. Ongoing and appropriate training and socialization also play their part in shaping how dogs react around other dogs, adults and, of course, children. Finally, even the most docile, good-natured dog can be pushed to their limit with children that are not respecting their space. Make sure you are an advocate for your dog and that you do not put them in situations with children that could be asking for trouble.

American Water Spaniel

The American Water Spaniel was developed in the Great Lakes region of the United States in the mid-1800s as a versatile hunting dog. These dogs excel at flushing and retrieving birds, and are comfortable both in the field and in the water. The breed is a little standoffish with strangers and needs socialization and training in puppyhood to develop into a confident and well-manned adult dog. American Water Spaniels are hard workers and have energy to spare, so they need lots of daily exercise to prevent behavior issues stemming from boredom. The upside to all this energy is that these dogs are happy to romp and play fetch as the kids keep throwing the ball or Frisbee. One of the rarer spaniels, the midsize American Water Spaniel is an energetic and merry companion, completely devoted to its human family, including children.

Breed Overview

HEIGHT: 15 to 18 inches tall at the shoulder

WEIGHT: 25 to 45 pounds

PHYSICAL CHARACTERISTICS:
Active, muscular and medium-sized; the thick double coat, which is wavy or tightly curled, comes in three shades of brown; solid liver, brown or dark chocolate.

Boykin Spaniel

Another rare spaniel that originated in the United States (South Carolina to be specific), the brown Boykin Spaniel is an enthusiastic hunting dog when in the field, but sweet and laid back at home. The breed was originally used to hunt wild turkeys, but today is prized for hunting smaller birds like ducks and doves. Friendly and playful, Boykins love being included in family activities, and get along great with respectful children, especially older kids who can throw the ball and play in the yard. Boykin Spaniels are very rare, so be prepared to get on a waitlist if you're hoping for a puppy.

Breed Overview

HEIGHT: 14 to 18 inches tall at the shoulder

WEIGHT: 30 to 40 pounds (males); 25 to 35 pounds (females)

PHYSICAL CHARACTERISTICS: Solidly built with moderate bone; the solid liver (brown) coat can range from flat to slightly wavy to curly, and is medium length

Brittany

Larger than a spaniel but smaller than a pointer or setter, the Brittany (sometimes incorrectly called the Brittany Spaniel) is a popular and versatile hunting, pointing and retrieving dog.

Brittanys are exceptionally friendly, willing to please, and are easily trained. They make great family dogs and are always ready and willing to join in on the next adventure. This could include hunting, hiking, running, swimming, camping and training for a competitive dog sport like agility. Because Brittanys have abundant energy, it's important to provide enough exercise and mental stimulation or they may become destructive or try to escape your yard.

Breed Overview

WEIGHT: 30 to 40 pounds

HEIGHT: 17.5 to 20.5 inches tall at the shoulder

PHYSICAL CHARACTERISTICS: Compact and leggy with a dense, flat or wavy coat in combinations of white and orange or reddish-brown

Bulldog

Dignified and even-tempered, the Bulldog is known for its affinity for children. These dogs are patient and docile, happily going along with calm play. Although Bulldogs are very tolerant, children should never be allowed to pester the dog or play too rough. Teach kids how to respect the dog's space and interact gently. Despite its heavy build, the Bulldog is also surprisingly active, enjoying long walks and romps in a safely enclosed area like your backyard. Many Bulldogs also love to chase after balls and toys—an excellent way for kids and dogs to play together. Take care not to exercise your Bulldog in hot weather. Due to the breed's pushed-in face, the Bulldog can overheat easily.

Breed Overview

HEIGHT: 14 to 15 inches tall at the shoulder

WEIGHT: 40 to 50 pounds

PHYSICAL CHARACTERISTICS: A heavy, thick-set, low-swung body and massive, short-faced head; the straight, short, fine-textured coat comes in red, white, fawn or fallow (pale brown), or any combination of these colors

English Springer Spaniel

Full of energy and exceedingly playful, the English Springer Spaniel is a great companion for kids. Excellent dogs for active families, Springers needs lots of daily exercise. Fom long walks to jogging, hiking, swimming, games of fetch or even training for a competitive sport like agility or flyball, your ESS will be up for the challenge. These dogs don't do well when left alone for long periods of time, but luckily their medium size makes it easy to take them along on family outings. The

Springer's coat requires professional grooming, and brushing a few times a week to keep mats at bay.

Breed Overview

HEIGHT: 19 to 20 inches tall at the shoulder

WEIGHT: 40 to 50 pounds

PHYSICAL CHARACTERISTICS: Compact, well-proportioned, muscular body; the medium-length double coat (a flat or wavy topcoat and a short, soft undercoat) is usually black or liver with white markings, or the opposite

Finnish Lapphund

The Finnish Lapphund is a spitz breed, a type of dog that hails from cold and snowy regions and has a fluffy coat, upright triangular ears and a tail that curls up and over the back. These types of dogs have been in existence for thousands of years in the northernmost region of Finland, where they were most recently used a reindeer herders. Lappies, as they are often called, have a friendly and submissive demeanor that makes the breed excellent for families with children. However, as with all breeds, care must be taken ensure the kids are gentle and kind in their interaction. Lappies love to play—toss a ball in the backyard and offer daily walks to keep them happy.

Breed Overview

HEIGHT: 16 to 21 inches tall at the shoulder

WEIGHT: 33 to 53 pounds

PHYSICAL CHARACTERISTICS: Strongly built and thickly coated;

the double-coat comes in black, golden, brown, cream, wolfsable and white

Icelandic Sheepdog

The only native breed to Iceland, the fluffy Icelandic Sheepdogs history dates back more than 1,000 years. The breed was used to watch over and herd livestock like sheep, cattle and horses. The Icelandic Sheepdog is another spitz breed (also referred to as Northern breeds), easily identified by its foxy-looking face, triangle ears, fluffy coat, and plumed tail curling over its back.

Friendly and affectionate, Icelandic Sheepdogs are mostly beloved family pets these days, though they still retain a strong instinct to herd. They are lively, confident, curious, and enjoy playing with respectful children. Icelandic Sheepdogs are sturdy enough for gentle play, yet small enough that they won't accidentally knock down small children. The breed is rare, so if you think you might be interested in a puppy, prepare to wait.

Breed Overview

HEIGHT: 16.5 to 18 inches tall at the shoulder

WEIGHT: 25 to 30 pounds

PHYSICAL CHARACTERISTICS: Rectangular, medium-sized spitz breed; the thick, waterproof double coat can be short or long, and comes in a variety of colors, including fawn, cream, chocolate, black and gray

Keeshond

Another spitz breed, the Keeshond stands out with its unique black glasses-shaped markings around the eyes. Though found throughout Europe for many centuries, the breed was most popular in Holland, where they were used as watchdogs on riverboats, barges and farms. Friendly, spirited and outgoing, the Keeshond is renowned as an outstanding family dog. They are especially gentle and empathetic and make wonderful therapy dogs. This breed is active and needs daily exercise and play, but what it wants most is to spend time with the family. The fluffy coat, which feels clean and has very little doggie odor, needs a good weekly brushing and bathing every month or two.

Staffordshire Bull Terrier

Famous for its affection toward people and its special affinity for children, the Staffordshire Bull Terrier has earned the nicknames "Children's Nursemaid" and "Nanny Dog." Of course, this is not to say that this breed should be left home alone to babysit the kids, but with proper adult supervision, kids and Staffies can be the very best of friends. The Staffordshire Bull Terrier is small but mighty, with a muscular body and brave temperament. Although Staffies love people, many do not get along well with other dogs, especially strange dogs. Some have very high prey drive (the instinct to chase), and the breed is not considered trustworthy around small pets like cats.

Breed Overview

HEIGHT: 14 to 16 inches tall at the shoulder

WEIGHT: 24 to 38 pounds

PHYSICAL CHARACTERISTICS: Active, agile and of great strength for its size; the short, smooth coat comes in red, fawn, white, black, blue or brindle (any shade), with or without white.

Whippet

The Whippet is a sighthound, which is a type of hound that hunts using its excellent eyesight and speed. Quiet, gentle and mellow, the Whippet is made for family life. The breed is known for being tolerant and kind and for enjoying the company of children as long as the kids are gentle and respectful. If you provide daily opportunities for brief sprints, Whippets are generally very laidback in the house—some may even call them lazy. Whippets are prone to escape attempts and will chase anything that moves (cats, squirrels, even wind-blown leaves or trash), even if that is into the street and oncoming cars. To avoid heartbreak, keep your doors secured and keep your Whippet on a leash when outside or ensure off-leash exercise is always in a safely enclosed area.

Breed Overview

HEIGHT: 18 to 22 inches tall at the shoulder

WEIGHT: 25 to 40 pounds

PHYSICAL CHARACTERISTICS: Medium-sized, with balanced muscular power and strength; the short, smooth coat in a variety of colors including black, blue, fawn, red, white, and various shades of brindle

How to Stop Your Dog From Fearing the Veterinarian

Fear of going to see the vet is a common anxiety in dogs. Even the most happy-go-lucky canine may cower and tuck its tail as you try to coax it through the door of your veterinarian's office. While your dog might never learn to love a trip to visit the veterinarian, there are steps you can take to assuage some of the anxiety your pet feels when it senses a vet visit is imminent.

Why Do Dogs Fear the Vet?

The most common reason that dogs develop a fear of going to the veterinarian is that it feels traumatic to them.1? Think about a typical visit to the vet's office with your dog. As soon as you walk through the door, your dog is bombarded by strange smells and sounds. Chances are you'll run into other animals while you're there, which can certainly raise your dog's anxiety level as well. Next comes the examination. Your dog is restrained by a veterinary technician while the veterinarian pokes and prods it, possibly giving vaccinations and drawing blood. This unfamiliar type of handling by strangers can cause your dog to become confused and afraid. If your dog is sick or injured, it's already feeling bad. Add it all together and you get a pretty traumatic experience for your dog.

It's no wonder so many dogs develop a fear of going to the vet.

How to Stop the Fear

The good news is that a dog's fear of the veterinarian is fairly easy to prevent or conquer if you're willing to put in the necessary time and effort. Even if the fear isn't completely eradicated, it's possible to ease a lot of your dog's anxiety. Eventually, you may even be able to get your dog to love the vet. Try a few approaches to help make your dog's next checkup a lot easier for both of you, but keep in mind that depending on how severe the anxiety is, you may need to involve your vet in finding the right solution.

Practice Exams at Home

Part of what makes visits to the veterinarian so scary is that your dog isn't used to the handling it receives during an exam. You can get your dog used to this type of handling by practicing at home.2?

Spend some time each day checking its ears, restraining it, looking at its teeth, and holding its paws. Be gentle and make sure your dog gets lots of praise and some treats during the practice exams.

Visit the Vet's Office Socially

The only time some dogs see the vet is when they're sick or it's time for their vaccinations. Try to make arrangements with your veterinarian's office to stop by several times for nothing more than a social call. Ask the receptionist to give your dog a few treats and some friendly petting, and soon your dog may look forward to visiting the vet. Gently practice going into the vet's office during social visits and don't force your dog. Let it take its time getting comfortable with the idea, rather than dragging or carrying it in. Reward your dog with lots of treats and praise as it edges closer to going through the door.

Medicate for Anxiety

Although many people consider it a last resort, some dogs are so fearful of the vet that medication is the only option. Your vet may be able to prescribe an anti-anxiety drug that you give your dog at home before visits to the office. For milder cases, anxiety-relieving nutritional supplements, pheromone preparations, and other products may be helpful. You can also use this as a tool to practice social visits and handling. It's important to understand that a dog is incapable of learning new things when it's in a state of high anxiety. Medication can help bring the fear and anxiety down to a level where the dog can respond to training and socialization and may not be needed permanently.

Use a Muzzle

If your dog's fear is so strong that it results in aggression, you may want to consider using a muzzle during trips to the vet to prevent a dog bite. Get your dog used to the muzzle slowly at home by having it wear the muzzle regularly and being lavished with praise. If you wait until you're about to leave for an appointment before introducing your dog to the muzzle, it may quickly associate the muzzle with the vet and develop a fear of the muzzle. Make the experience as positive as possible.

Find a Vet Who Makes House Calls or a Fear-Free Clinic

More and more veterinarians are willing to come to your home for routine exams and vaccinations. You may be able to ease your dog's fears by making it comfortable in its own home during examinations. Search for mobile vets with good reviews that are in your area.

Some veterinary hospitals go the extra mile when it comes to relieving their patient's anxiety. The doctors and staff at Fear-Free Veterinary Clinics have "taken the time to complete extra behavioral and fear-free practice training/certification to help aid fearful pets."

Get Additional Help

It's important for you to understand that your dog won't immediately get over being afraid of the vet no matter what steps you take, so exercise patience and be consistent. Talk to your vet for help with this situation. The vet and her staff truly want to help you and your dog, but communication is essential. If you and your vet can't get your dog past its fear, it may be time to get assistance from a dog trainer or behaviorist.

How to Train Your Dog to Accept a New Baby

Welcoming a new baby into the family is exciting. It can also be stressful, especially if you already have a dog. Hopefully, you've spent the last few months preparing the dog for the baby's arrival. Even if you haven't thought of it before now, there are several things you can do to make the introduction between your dog and newborn go smoothly. None of these techniques are hard, but do be patient and consistent with your dog.

Bring Home Baby's Blanket

After your baby is born, but before bringing your new family member home from the hospital, bring home a blanket or article of clothing the baby has been wrapped in. Allow your dog to sniff and explore the blanket at its own pace. By the time you bring your newborn home, your dog should be somewhat familiar with the baby's scent.

Your Baby in While the Dog Is Outside

Chances are your dog is going to be very excited when its female owner walks through the door with the new baby. Aside from the new bundle of unfamiliar smells and sounds, your pup probably hasn't seen "mom" for at least a day or so. The dog is bound to be excited when you walk through the door. Try having someone get to your home before you get there. Have them take the dog out for a long walk or playtime so it can burn off some excess energy. Wait until you and baby are settled comfortably before you bring your dog in to welcome the new arrival.

Allow the Dog to Say Hello to Mom First

Before bringing the dog into the same room as the baby, allow the dog to have some time to say hello to the new mother first. If the new mom walks in holding the baby, an excited dog may jump up to say hello. The first reaction may be to scold the dog for fear of harming the newborn. This can start the introductions off on the wrong foot. Instead, allow your dog to greet you before bringing the baby into the mix.

Keep Control of the Dog

For the initial meeting between the dog and baby, one person should hold the baby while the other has control of the dog. Keep the dog on the leash while you bring it over to say hello. Don't force the dog to approach the baby, but be sure to give the pup lots of praise and encouragement for approaching calmly. If it gets too excited and pulls on the leash to rush to the baby, the person holding the dog should back up and start again. Take a few slow steps at a time and reward when the dog goes slowly and remains calm.

Tell Your Dog What You Want

Instead of waiting to see if your dog is going to try to jump up or greet the baby too exuberantly or with aggression, let the dog know how you expect it to behave. As your dog approaches the new baby, give it a command, such as "down" or "sit." Reward the dog with praise or treats for doing as its told. Often, your dog just needs some direction from you to learn how to be well-behaved around an infant.

Maintain Your Dog's Schedule

One of the reasons many dogs behave badly when a new baby is brought home is because they get stressed at all the changes taking place in the house. You can greatly reduce your dog's stress simply by sticking to its regular schedule. Try to make sure the dog gets fed and walked at the same times it always did before the baby came home. It can be tough when you're trying to juggle your dog's schedule with that of a newborn, but it will be well worth the effort when your dog and baby develop a positive relationship. Help from friends and family can make things go easier.

Never Leave a Dog and Baby Unsupervised

This point cannot be stated strongly enough. Don't put your baby and your dog in a bad position by leaving them alone together. Accidents can happen even with the most well-behaved dogs. Prevent mishaps by never leaving your baby unattended in a room with the dog.

Problems and Proofing Behavior

A common mistake is to expect your dog to love your baby just as much as you do. Give your dog time. The baby (along with the visitors, new routine, etc.) are a big change for your dog. If your dog seems to be acting especially aggressive toward you or the baby, speak to your vet as soon as possible. This is an uncomfortable (and potentially dangerous) situation that you want to get sorted out quickly. If your dog reacts too exuberantly when it's first introduced to the new baby, try to resist the temptation to scold the pup or to give it a leash correction. You don't want your dog to associate the baby with anything negative. Instead, use some treats to lure the dog away from the baby, give the dog some attention and some time to calm down, and then bring it back to try again. Keep some tasty treats on hand for the first few days or so after bringing baby home. Try to remember to give your dog some treats and praise any time it is remaining calm and well-behaved when the baby is nearby. This will teach your dog that having the baby around means good things happen.

Why Dogs Jump up and Down and How to Stop It

Not only are dogs jumping on you generally annoying, but it can also be dangerous for people who aren't as steady on their feet. It can make people very mad at your dog.

Since dogs don't use the same language we do, they cannot communicate with us in the same way. So we have to look at their actions and behaviors as their method of communication.

Dogs Jump to Say Hello

If you have ever seen two dogs when they meet, they greet each other face to face, unless there is a massive size disparity. So, why are we surprised when that is how a dog wants to greet us? You come home from work and let your dog out, and they are excited to see you and excited to show you how much they have missed you. So they jump up on you to get closer and give you some love.

How to Stop Dogs From Jumping to Say Hello

To stop this type of jumping, you need to be prepared before your dog is let out or gets to you. Your dog will take its cues from your body language and how you start the interaction. This means there are two ways to go here: do you want your dog to be invited to jump up, or do you want it to keep all four paws on the floor?

If you want your dog to jump, you have to work on that when it is less excited. The good thing is that it is usually pretty easy to get most dogs to jump.

Get a couple of treats that your dog loves.

- Take your dog to a nice open place where it can get a little excited.

- Have your dog sit in front of you calmly, wearing its leash.
- Tell it "hug" or "give me a hug" or whatever command you'd like to use here and pat on your lap to get your dog to jump up.
- Be prepared for either an awkward look from your dog that says, "Dude, you don't usually want me to jump on you. Is this a trick?" Or, a full four paw jump, because they are so excited you finally understand its need to jump on you!

- When your dog has jumped up and is being a little calmer about it, verbally praise it and give them a snack. Then, in a clear and strong tone, tell them, "off," while moving into them with your body (not pushing them off with your hands).

- If it comes back to jump on you again, say, "off," and move into it again. If your dog refuses to listen to that, step on the leash so that it is not able to jump up.

- Continue to repeat this 2 or 3 times during each training session, a couple of times a day until it understands both "hug" and "off."

If you do not want your dog to jump up, follow these steps:

- As your dog is approaching to jump, move towards and lean your upper body over your dog as you say "off."
- If your dog does not respond, then practice this when it is

calmer. Also, work on respect exercises and training.

- Use your leash by stepping on it, so that your dog doesn't have the space to jump on you until it calms down.

- Work on the above steps of teaching a command to jump up so that your dog understands that there is a difference. Sometimes teaching a command to do an annoying behavior is exactly what will make your dog stop.

Dogs Jump to Establish Control and Dominance

Since dogs don't have language skills like we do to work out issues, they have to figure things out in a different way. They do that with their body language and space usage to work out pack rankings. Determining if this is your dog is a little more complicated, but it is often seen when your dog isn't very excited (or that there isn't much of a reason to be excited). This is more than likely to happen when you are in their way or have something that they want. They will usually jump on you and try to push you back more than just jumping up to give you kisses. Often times they will jump on you and try to hold on when you push them away or try to move into them. Sometimes moving into them may elicit a growl because they want to back you off.

How to Stop Dogs From Jumping to Establish Control and Dominance

Jumping to establish control is a different thing from an excited dog just trying to say hello. This dog is showing you that it does not respect you and that it believes that you don't need to be listened to. So the work needed to stop this behavior is all about building respect and doing a bit more training. The first thing you need to do is calmly accept what your dog is telling you, and decide today to make a change in how you interact with your dog. Note: if your dog has growled at you or tried to bite you when you move into it, please seek professional help in your area to help solve this issue.

 Building a foundation of respect in a dog is not hard; it just takes consistency and perseverance. A couple of things you can easily do starting today:

- Make your dog wait at every doorway and threshold you cross so that you go first and claim the territory. If your dog is one that always wants to dart through first, use your leash to stop it.

- Have your dog sit and wait for its food before it is allowed to eat.

- Start working on backup, where you move into your dog and have them back up from you.

- These items take time and practice, but your dog will respond if you are consistent and dedicated to making the change.

Dogs Jump out of Fear or to Alert

This type of jumping is the one that you need to pay attention to the most in your life with your dog. If you have a dog that rarely ever jumps on you, and all of a sudden they jump up and put their paws on you, it may be time to pay close attention to your dog. If a dog is stressed or afraid, their demeanor and typical behaviors will change. If you see this in your dog (or really any dog you know) you should step back and check on your dog. Are they hurt? Did a new dog come around they don't know? Has the weather changed? Is it hot outside? When was the last time they had a chance to go outside to pee or poop? Look closely at your dog and figure out what kind of thing is stressing them. Please don't dismiss their change in behavior. They have turned to you to beg for something and don't know another way to tell you.

How to Stop Dogs From Fearful or Alerting Jumping

You shouldn't stop this type of jumping. You need to diagnose your dog's issue and remedy that. If your dog is just stressed being in a new situation, you should calmly get them off of you, offer them a treat to calm them down, and have them sit politely beside you until their stress level has subsided (or take them somewhere else so that they can calm down if it is taking a while for them to calm down.) But most of all, please do not just ignore this behavior change.

Dogs Jump Due to Poor Social Skills

Having a dog with poor social skills is a balancing act. It's about getting them to experience new places, balancing their stress levels, and just letting them experience new things so that they can get used to all of it. Dogs with poor social skills oftentimes just don't know better. They will bounce off of everything, jump on everyone, run around like crazy, and investigate everything they can get their paws, snout, and eyes on! These dogs can come from any background, whether a rescue or puppy from a great breeder; if they haven't had experience in new places and new situations, this can be how they respond.

How to Stop Dogs With Poor Social Skills From Jumping

A dog with poor social skills is one of the hardest dogs to stop jumping. They are like a 4-year-old at Chuck E. Cheese for the first time. They won't be able to hear you or comprehend what you are saying because they are so overstimulated. So, our job is to redirect them and gently show them the right things to be doing.

For a dog with poor social skills?, the leash is your tool of choice.

Your job is to slow down this dog and get their focus back.

Use treats if your dog will take them, to get its focus back on you.

Using the leash, get your dog to do a few basic commands and start working for you. This will help center it and get some focus on a simple task.

Take the dog away from the situation that is over-stimulating it.

Once it has calmed down, bring it back into the situation, this time keeping it focused on you.

Use the steps of an excited dog say hi to teach your dog "Hug" and "Off" so that it can become second nature.

A dog jumping on you can be an annoying thing, but there are different things to look at to determine how to handle the problem.

How to Stop Your Dog From Jumping Up

Jumping up is a common behavior problem among dogs. You may be annoyed by your excited, overly exuberant dog attacking you the minute you step through the front door. But it can actually be dangerous for small children, people who have physical disabilities, some older people, and people who aren't expecting your dog's greeting. The good news is that you can train your dog to stop jumping on people and start greeting everyone more politely.

Why Do Dogs Jump Up?

There are a number of theories about why dogs jump up on people; popular among these are dominance and greeting behaviors. The truth is, though, that your dog is probably jumping up to say, "Look at me!" You might inadvertently be rewarding your dog for jumping up on you by giving it what it wants. As is often true of kids, negative attention may be better than no attention. Your dog doesn't necessarily realize that when you push it off or yell at it to get down that you're attempting to punish it. Instead, your pup may view your behavior as exactly what it's seeking: treasured attention from you. In this case, any type of attention that the dog gets from you or others may be perceived as a reward. It makes sense then that instead of rewarding your dog for jumping up, you make it more rewarding for it to keep all four paws on the floor.

How to Stop the Jumping Up

Training your dog not to jump up on people takes patience and persistence on your part. Be aware that there are actions that you should take and others that you should avoid. Be consistent when you're training your dog, and you'll be rewarded with a best friend who keeps its front paws to itself.

Withhold Attention

The first part of teaching a dog not to jump up involves withholding your attention. There are a couple of ways to do this:

As soon as your dog jumps up, turn your back. Cross your arms over your chest and don't make a sound. If the dog runs around to jump up again, turn the other way. Wait for the dog to stop jumping.

Another method is to remove yourself altogether. If your dog jumps up when you walk in the door, turn around and walk back outside. If it jumps up when you're inside, walk out of the room. Wait a moment; then step back inside. Repeat this until your dog calms down.

Reward Good Behavior

When you're working on preventing unwanted jumping, it can really help to keep some treats close at hand. As soon as your dog is standing in front of you with all four paws on the ground, toss it a treat. Praise your dog as well, but keep things low key. Too much excitement and attention from you may stimulate another round of jumping.

Practice Makes Perfect

It helps if you can set up situations to practice with your dog. For instance, if the jumping occurs most often when you come home after work, spend a few minutes several times a day coming and going. Don't make a big fuss over your dog and step back outside if it jumps up. Offer a reward anytime all four feet are simultaneously on the floor.

Add a Sit Command

Once your dog is able to keep four paws on the floor for a few seconds or more, start asking it to sit. Walk into a room or through the front door and give the command "sit." As soon as the dog sits, offer a treat. Practice this over several training sessions. With plenty of repetitions, your dog will start sitting as soon as you walk through the door or enter the room.

Practice With Other People

It's not enough that you practice with your dog. You should also involve friends and family in this training. Otherwise, your dog may learn that it's not OK to jump up on you but everyone else is fair game. Having other people help with this training teaches your dog to keep all four paws down no matter who comes into the room.

What Not to Do

You may have heard about methods of training a dog not to jump that call for some form of punishment or aversive. One such method is a knee to the dog's chest. Another is using leash correction—pulling or yanking on the leash—to get the dog off you. There are several problems with these methods:

If you knee or leash correct your dog too harshly or improperly, you can seriously injure the dog.

When you use a knee to the chest, you may knock your dog down, but the dog may interpret this as your way of initiating play. Your dog's response will likely be to jump up again to continue the game because you've actually reinforced the behavior you're trying to stop.

Your dog may learn not to jump up only when it's on ?a leash. Since most dogs aren't leashed 24/7, chances are your dog will have plenty of opportunities to get away with jumping up when it's off its leash.

What to Expect in the First 24 Hours With Your New Dog

From the cuddles to the cuteness, welcoming a new four-legged family member into your home is certainly an exciting time. However, that isn't to say that those first hours with a new dog (or a new baby for that matter) don't come with their own unique challenges. There's accidents and sleep deprivation and, much like becoming mom and dad to a human baby, many pet parents will wonder if they're "doing it right." Here's what to do in those first 24 hours to help ease the transition for both the human and canine members of your family.

Let them Settle In

Within the first few hours after your dog's arrival, you'll want to make sure that they have everything they'll need to make your house feel like a forever home. Have the basic necessities already stocked, like: The last thing you'll want to do is make a run to the nearest pet store when your dog is just getting used to their new environment (and people). You'll also want to make an effort to keep those early hours calm and relaxed. Keep visitors to a minimum while your pup has peace and quiet for napping and exploring their new digs. Encourage younger children to lay low for a day or two and give the dog some privacy to prevent the dog from getting overwhelmed, and keep other pets away from your new pup until they're more acclimated. Be aware that your new adorable pup could sleep up to 20 hours a day, and as soon as they wake, they'll probably need a bathroom break, so prepare to take off work for a few days.

Potty Training

When they're not sleeping (or sniffing), one of the first things you'll want to do is introduce your new family member to their potty area. Whether it's a specific section of grass out front, your fenced-in backyard, or you plan to use an indoor wee-wee pad, potty training should begin within minutes of your pet's arrival. For new puppies, set an alarm to head to the "potty" every two hours or so. Even if you've adopted an older, previously house-trained dog, it's likely that there are still going to be some accidents as they acclimate to their new surroundings. The sooner you can establish a routine—and get into the practice of heaping lots of praise (and treats!) on your pet for doing their business outside—the faster you'll be on your way to a potty-trained pooch.

Setting Simple Boundaries

Much like potty training, those first few hours your dog is home is also the prime opportunity to teach your furry friend the house rules. Don't want your puppy chewing on the furniture? You'll have to keep a watchful eye on your mischievous pup to catch them in the act and interrupt the misbehavior. That's the best time to introduce an exciting new toy and offer lots of praise for chewing on a bone instead of your dining room table.

Introduce Pet-Friendly Zones

After the first few hours, you might find yourself needing to get things done around the house or take a break from the 24-hour supervision that a new dog requires. That's where a crate, gate, or playpen comes in handy. You'll want to take time to introduce your dog to any pet-friendly zones you've prepared for them. Outfit their special areas with a dog bed, blanket, toys, and any other cozy additions to make them feel at home. Since you've already started establishing daily routines, acquainting your pooch to their section of the family room or a guest bedroom is a great thing to do after they're done exploring the house—and if you haven't already, now is a good time to pet-proof any other areas of the home that they seemed to take an interest in, such as closets with your favorite shoes. After they've been home for a few hours, get all of the members of the family down on the floor to engage in some quality play-time to begin a positive association. If you'll be feeding your dog in the kitchen, serve them a meal in the place where they will now be dining. If you'll be taking your dog for a leashed walk around the neighborhood or letting them burn off some energy in their new backyard, that they are constantly supervised and prevented from letting their curiosity and excitement put them in danger.

Get Some Sleep

Plan to hit the hay a little earlier than normal—much like a new baby, a puppy will likely prevent you from sleeping much those first nights. Even an older dog may feel scared or uncertain in their new surroundings (so don't be overly alarmed by whining or crying in the wee hours of the night), and they might need a few potty breaks throughout the night. Many pet owners have their dog's crate set up in their bedroom to provide that physical closeness and reassurance—as well as fast access to the outdoors when needed—and you'll want to be sure to make their crate as comfortable as possible with bedding, a blanket, or even a soft plush toy (assuming the dog can be trusted not to tear it to shreds). Whenever possible, you may also want to provide something that reminds a puppy of their mother, such as a blanket or towel that they used before you took them home, or even some of the mother's bedding if you're able to take it home from the breeder. No matter what your new dog's age, taking these steps to help them feel at home—while still establishing some boundaries and house rules—can make those first 24 hours with your new four-legged family member feel like a walk in the park.

Top 10 Tips for Childproofing a Dog

Dogs and children can be a great combination if your dog has learned how to behave around kids. Some dogs love children and seem to naturally know how to act around them. These dogs still need training and socialization. It's important that they know their boundaries. Not all dogs will get along with kids. In fact, some dogs are even afraid of children. Many of these dogs can be trained to behave around kids at a safe distance, but some will never be able to safely interact? with them. If you have children living in or visiting your home, it's vital to ensure they are always safe around your dog.

Socialize Your Puppy

Puppies go through a critical period of development between the ages of about 8 and 16 weeks. They are more likely to learn to accept and be comfortable with a variety of people and situations if they are introduced to them during this time. If you have a new puppy, introduce it to children in a positive way. Make sure it meets different children of various ages in a variety of situations. The children should be well-behaved around dogs and gentle. If your dog has good experiences with kids, it will associate them with good feelings. If you have an adult dog, you can still socialize it around kids. The process should go more slowly and gently. Make sure to offer plenty of valuable treats and praise. Remove your dog from the situation at the first sign of stress.

Start an Obedience Program

Having a well-behaved dog is the first step in ensuring the safety of children in your home. Teach your dog basic commands, such as sit and down, and you will be able to teach it how to behave around kids. For example, if its first impulse is to jump up to kiss visitors, teaching it to lie down instead will allow you to direct it to more appropriate behavior. You may wish to take your dog to training classes to get assistance from professional trainers. Dog training classes are more affordable than one-on-one professional training and allow your dog to learn to behave around other dogs.

Practice Handling Exercises

Even the most well-behaved child sometimes can't keep itself from throwing their arms around a dog's neck or tugging on a dog's tail. Prepare your dog for this kind of attention before it runs into a child. Give it lots of praise and maybe even a few treats while you gently pull its tail, hold its paws, hug it, and check out its ears. If your dog exhibits fear or anxiety at this gentle prodding, then it may be best to keep the kids at a distance.

Don't Allow Your Dog to Jump Up

You may not mind your dog jumping up on you to say hello, but not every visitor to your home will feel the same way. It can be especially dangerous when your visitor is a young child who can be injured if your dog knocks them over. Your best bet is not to allow your dog to jump up at all. If your dog jumps up when you walk through the door, you can ask it to sit instead. If this doesn't work, try walking right back out the door when it jumps. Give your dog lots of attention and praise for keeping all four paws on the floor when you walk through the door. The dog will soon learn that it's far more rewarding not to jump up on people.

Introduce Dogs to Children's Toys

Think about all the things children's toys can do. Dolls and stuffed animals often make funny, high-pitched noises. Bikes go whizzing by at a quick pace. Balls get tossed or kicked across the yard. All of these things can make it very tempting for your dog to steal, chew, or chase toys. While this can lead to toys being destroyed, it can also lead to children getting nipped or knocked over. Sensitive dogs may be afraid of some children's toys and then start to associate that fear with children as well. Introduce your dog to kids' toys without the kids around. This is when commands such as leave it and stay come in handy. Use these commands to keep your dog from stealing or chasing after toys. Be sure to redirect your dog to appropriate dog toys. If your dog is the nervous type, reward with treats when your dog is around the toys.

Act Like a Kid

Let's face it; kids behave differently than adults. They run and yell and move erratically. Try to introduce your dog to some of these behaviors yourself. Teach your dog to stay, and slowly work up to having it stay in one spot while you run around your yard or yell in a high-pitched, child-like voice. You can also get your dog used to the way children behave by taking him to a park or playground. Keep your distance at first, and slowly work your way closer to the playing children. If your dog seems concerned at any point, take a few steps back and start over. Keep things fun, and use lots of praise and treats.

Crate Train Your Dog

Dogs often do better around children if they have an escape route. Crate train your dog so that it is happy and comfortable in a crate. Make it clear to any children in your home that the crate is off-limits to them. This way your dog can interact with the children when it wants to, but it also has a safe place to take a break.

Don't Force a Dog to Accept Children

Some people think that holding a dog so a child can pet it is a good way to introduce dogs and kids. Not true! If a dog is afraid of children, holding it while a child approaches and pets it can be a terrifying experience. A dog who is afraid can become aggressive and growl, snap or bite in an effort to escape from the object of its fears—in this case, children. Instead allow your dog as much time as it needs to get comfortable around kids, and give it the chance to approach its own terms.

Keep It Positive

The best way to build a good relationship between your dog and children is to use positive reinforcement. When your dog is behaving well around children, be sure to give it lots of praise, treats, and attention. Your dog will learn that good things happen whenever kids are around. Soon it'll be happily seeking out children and keeping on its best behavior.

Give Children Rules

Dogs are not the only ones who need training. Children also need to be given rules about how to behave around your dog.

Be sure any child who enters your home knows the following:

The dog should be pet gently.

Attention should not be forced on the dog.

The dog's crate is off-limits.

Don't approach the dog while it is eating or chewing a bone.

Leave the dog alone while it is sleeping.

Make sure an adult is around when the dog is in the room. Children should never, ever be left unattended with a dog.

CONCLUSION

The definition of a stay requires that the dog remain in the designated place and position, with no resistance such as moving, whining, or barking, until you either release him or give another command. This is a fairly easy exercise to train, as it requires that the dog do nothing except remain doing nothing and stay in that spot for the length of time you indicate. However, dogs being what they are, they sometimes have problems executing exercises for which they see no purpose and do not especially enjoy. We can never make the stays particularly fun, but we can impress upon the dog the fact that we consider them important, and that the quicker the dog successfully accomplishes the assignment, the sooner it will be over. Have you ever had a dog break a stay that was really important to you? That could be in a competition situation or simply in a daily living activity. Sometimes the stay is the difference between being a safe, well-controlled companion and not. Do you really want solid stays in your ring work? Do you want a dog who will remain in a certain position, regardless of where you are, until you release him? In either case, you must impress upon the dog the absolute importance of this exercise and the total futility of attempting to escape doing it. Before we start to train, it is important for you to understand the dog's point of view. The best way to do that is to have an insight into how you think. If you ever played any game of chance, you will get this quickly. It is the principle that makes casinos rich. When you pull that lever on a slot machine and win once, the odds are you will continue to repeatedly pull it, even though you do not win for a long time before you give up. If occasionally you win, however, you'll keep playing for even longer. This process involves the mechanism of variable-reinforcement training, which is the method by which we train with food on a continuous routine and then remove the food so the dog will continue to perform for a long time with only occasional food rewards. The occasional-reinforcement system is a very powerful motivator for continued behavior. Taking that into account, here's what you must internalize: If the dog gets up to come to you, he must not succeed—ever! Because if he makes it once, the urge to try for another "win" will last a long, long time. The dog carries an extremely high and well-developed desire to be with or near you. That desire takes precedent over most obedience commands that are given or require actions at a distance. This will be a factor throughout your training. Many good dogs are spoiled through corrections when from the dog's point of view, the only crime committed was trying to get back to the master he loves. Under these circumstances, there are some dogs and some breeds of dogs that can be emotionally damaged with certain aspects of force-training. However, a dog can learn to be away from the owner for certain periods of time without undue stress. You must do the exercise calmly, in short increments, giving the dog time to adjust to and internalize the learning experience as you go. Using a flat, plastic snap-collar and a 6- to 8-foot lead, take your dog up to a door with a secure knob and enough space around it for the dog to move, but not get into trouble. If you don't have one of those, find an opening in the house where you can lay a broomstick across the threshold and, again, have enough room so that if the dog moves around, there is nothing to entertain him or that he might destroy. You can slip the lead-handle over the stick or make a loop in it and secure it to the doorknob. Now, the dog can only walk to the end of the lead and no further.

The first step will be to put the dog on this, tell him to wait, and move away. When he tries to follow, he can't. You do nothing. Once he settles, you go back to him with a treat and loads of praise for a good wait. Repeat this until the dog is relaxed for up to a minute with you in the room, and then expand it until he is OK with you being out of sight. He can walk around, sit, lie down, or just stand there. If he makes any noise, ignore him until he is quiet, then quickly return and treat and praise him.

The next step is to get him standing back from the end of the lead a foot or so. With your hand open, give a stay command, say "stay," and step past the end of the lead about a foot. If the dog stays, step back, reward, and praise. Keep doing this, moving farther away as you progress. Most dogs will start toward you at some point. You do nothing. The dog will stop when he reaches the end of the lead. Go back, reposition him where he started, give the stay command and hand signal again and walk away. He may break several times before it sinks in that he can't get to you. If he moves, you are just going to reposition and repeat the stay command.

Once he stays a few seconds with you at the distance he was breaking, get back quickly to praise and reward. If he is like most dogs, he will learn that waiting for you to return is the quickest way to get you back to him, get his treat, then be done with that exercise for the bit. Do not speak to the dog when he breaks. Any negative tone in your voice is going to upset the dog and interfere with his ability to make the proper connections in this learning sequence. Stay calm. Think thoughts related to how smart the dog is, how important to you that he learn this sequence, how sure you are that he can do so, and how proud you are of him for trying. Think the same thoughts as he begins to understand and do the exercise correctly—only drop the "trying" part, and add how proud you are of him for succeeding. Dogs can pick up a great deal of what you are thinking. If not the actual words, at least the intent and emotions attached. This should become a very important element in all of your future communications with your dog, not just in training but also in everyday interactions.

As you progress, add the sit-stay and later the down-stay with the same technique. When you go away or outside to proof, have a light line already attached to something, with the snap end laying where you are going to put the dog for the stay. Walk over, on lead, then snap the lead off and the light line on. Proceed to practice, making sure that the end of the line is just a foot in front of where you are leaving the dog. You want it slack, but not enough for the dog to make more than a step or so. If there is no place to secure the line, have someone stand and hold the end. Make sure they are far enough behind the dog to not interfere with him. If you are faithful with this technique, your stays will be solid for a long, long time. It is well worth the time and effort spent when you consider the number of good dogs who never achieve the advanced titles because they learned to break the stays. It is one of the hardest exercises to fix if once broken in the ring. Follow this procedure carefully, and you will never have to deal with attempting the repair.